What color is it?

Bobbie Kalman

Crabtree Publishing Company

www.crabtreebooks.com

Created by Bobbie Kalman

Dedicated by Reagan Miller
For my sister Lyndsay, who brightens my world

**Author and
Editor-in-Chief**
Bobbie Kalman

Editors
Reagan Miller
Robin Johnson

Photo research
Crystal Sikkens

Design
Bobbie Kalman
Katherine Kantor
Samantha Crabtree (cover)

Production coordinator
Katherine Kantor

Illustrations
Barbara Bedell: pages 9, 24 (leaf and red bird)
Jeannette McNaughton-Julich: page 19 (skunk)
Vanessa Parson-Robbs: pages 18 (right penguin and left penguin beak),
    24 (penguin beak)
Bonna Rouse: page 19 (panda)
Margaret Amy Salter: pages 18 (left penguin except beak),
    24 (penguin except beak)

Photographs
© Dreamstime.com: pages 20 (top), 22
© iStockphoto.com: pages 5 (food rainbow), 6 (girl), 7 (top), 15 (top), 17 (top)
© ShutterStock.com: front cover, pages 1, 3, 4, 5 (grapes), 6 (border), 8, 9,
    10, 11, 12 (border), 13 (border and top right), 14, 15 (all except top),
    16, 17 (all except top), 18, 19, 20 (bottom), 21, 23, 24 (chick, frogs,
    paint colors, and flowers)
Other images by Comstock, Corbis, Digital Vision, Photodisc, and
    Tongro Image Stock

Library and Archives Canada Cataloguing in Publication

Kalman, Bobbie, 1947-
    What color is it? / Bobbie Kalman.

(Looking at nature)
Includes index.
ISBN 978-0-7787-3318-8 (bound).--ISBN 978-0-7787-3338-6 (pbk.)

    1. Colors--Juvenile literature. 2. Color in nature--Juvenile literature.
I. Title. II. Series: Looking at nature (St. Catharines, Ont.)

QC495.5.K36 2007   j535.6   C2007-904697-5

Library of Congress Cataloging-in-Publication Data

Kalman, Bobbie.
    What color is it? / Bobbie Kalman.
      p. cm. -- (Looking at nature)
    Includes index.
    ISBN-13: 978-0-7787-3318-8 (rlb)
    ISBN-10: 0-7787-3318-1 (rlb)
    ISBN-13: 978-0-7787-3338-6 (pb)
    ISBN-10: 0-7787-3338-6 (pb)
    1. Colors--Juvenile literature. 2. Color in nature--Juvenile literature.
I. Title. II. Series.

QC495.5.K35 2008
535.6--dc22
                          2007030177

Crabtree Publishing Company
www.crabtreebooks.com   1-800-387-7650

**Published in Canada
Crabtree Publishing**
616 Welland Ave.
St. Catharines, Ontario
L2M 5V6

**Published in the United States
Crabtree Publishing**
PMB16A
350 Fifth Ave., Suite 3308
New York, NY 10118

**Published in the United Kingdom
Crabtree Publishing**
White Cross Mills
High Town, Lancaster
LA1 4XS

**Published in Australia
Crabtree Publishing**
386 Mt. Alexander Rd.
Ascot Vale (Melbourne)
VIC 3032

Contents

A rainbow of colors

Colors come from sunlight. We can see the colors of sunlight in rainbows. The colors in rainbows are red, orange, yellow, green, blue, and purple.

red

orange

yellow

green

blue

purple

Our food comes in a rainbow of colors, too.

What color is a tomato?

What color is an orange?

What color are bananas?

What colors are apples?

What color are blueberries?

What colors are grapes?

What is red?

Some flowers are red.

Some fruits are, too.

Which red foods are liked by you?

What color are the eyes of these frogs? What color are the flowers on this page? Look at the frog below. Which part of the frog is the same color as grass?

Orange beauty

Orange butterflies sit on an orange flower. What is the name of these orange butterflies? Did you say monarch? The flower is called a tiger lily. Why do you think this flower is named after a tiger?

A tiger's fur is orange.

A tiger's stripes are black.

A tiger has a lot of stripes on its face, its tail, and its back.

The sun is yellow

What is in the sky that is
yellow, round, and hot?
Did you guess the sun,
or did you not?

The colors on this page are yellow,
orange, and red. These colors are
called **warm colors**. Why do you
think they are called warm?

On a yellow flower, sits a yellow bee. There is a yellow spider, too, but it is very hard to see. The bee is now the spider's food. Do you find that very rude?

bee

spider

It's a green world!

It is a beautiful green world out there. Green plants are growing everywhere. It is a beautiful world when we care. We must take care of this planet we share.

Little green tree frogs live in green rain forests.

Green leafy sea dragons live under water in oceans.

This green praying mantis lives on green plants.

Many kinds of snakes are green.

Cool blue

The sky is blue. The water is blue. What color are these leaves? Are they blue, too? Blue and green are called **cool colors**. Why do you think these colors are called cool?

Skies can be blue. Eyes can be blue.

Feet can be blue, too. These birds have blue feet.

That is why they are called blue-footed boobies.

15

Purple violets

"Roses are red. Violets are blue."
What color do these violets look to you?
Violet is another name for purple. Violet
is also the name of a flower. All these
flowers are violets. Which violets look
purple? Which violets look blue?

This purple crab
lives on the beach.

This purple octopus
lives in the ocean.

White and black

Snow is white. Ice is white.
Penguins live on snow and ice.
Penguins have white and black
feathers. Their thick feathers
keep them warm in their icy homes.

Zebras have white bodies with black stripes. Which other animals are white and black? Name the other black-and-white animals on this page.

panda

paper kite butterfly

skunk

baby chicks

zebra

dalmatian

Make some colors!

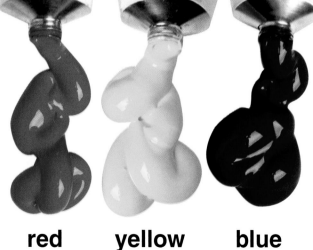

red   **yellow**   **blue**

You can make many colors using just three colors. These colors are called **primary colors**. What are the three primary colors? They are shown on the left.

Get some paint and mix these colors.

Red and yellow make orange.

Yellow and blue make green.

Blue and red make purple.

Yellow, blue, and red make brown.

Red and white make pink.

Colorful moods

People use color to show how they feel. Which color shows that you are sad? Which color shows that you are afraid? Which color shows that you are angry? Which color makes us feel happy? Which color means you are in a very bad mood?

This girl is wearing yellow. Is she afraid?

This girl is wearing a red shirt. Is she angry? She is wearing blue pants. Is she feeling sad?

This boy is wearing black. Is he in a very bad mood?

Which color makes us happy?

Words to know and Index

black
pages 9,
18-19, 23

blue
pages 4, 14-15,
16, 20, 21, 23

blue

green

cool colors
page 14

green
pages 4,
12-13,
14, 21

orange
pages 4, 8-9,
10, 21

**primary
colors**
page 20

violets

purple
pages 4,
16-17, 21

red
pages 4, 6-7, 10,
16, 20, 21, 23

red

orange

yellow

**warm
colors**
page 10

white
pages
18-19, 21

yellow
pages 4, 10-11,
20, 21, 23

Other index words

colorful moods
pages 22-23

food pages 5, 6, 11

making colors
pages 20-21

rainbows pages 4, 5

24

Printed in the U.S.A.